How To

This Is How You Do It

How To Train A Puppy

This Is How You Do It

By
Emily Pruitt

TABLE OF CONTENTS

CopyRight Info

Intro

Puppy Potty Training

How To Stop Puppy Biting

How To Stop Puppy Chewing

Leash Training A Puppy

Teaching Your Puppy To Heal

Teaching Your Puppy To Sit

Teaching Your Puppy To Lie Down

Teaching Your Puppy To Come

Teaching Your Puppy To Stay

In Closing

About the Author

CopyRight Info

Copyright 2012 Pruitt Farm
Pruitt Farm's Publishing Company
http://dogtrainingtipss.com/

All rights reserved.

No part of this publication may be copied, reproduced in any format, by any means, electronic or otherwise, without prior consent from the copyright owner and publisher of this book.

Intro

Contrary to what some of the dog training books on the market try to lead you to believe, you're not going to potty train your puppy in three days and you're not going to obedience train them in seven.

Puppies have short attention spans and small bladders and that is why I feel comfortable in making that bold claim and also why I believe that some, not all, but some of the books on the market today are trying to mislead you.

The methods outlined in this book are methods that we use. They work for us and they should work for you to. To potty train your puppy and teach them some of the basic obedience fundamentals will take some time but they will get there.

There is nothing better than a well trained dog. Even a dog or pup that understands the basics is much better and more enjoyable to be around than one that doesn't.

The best piece of advice that we can offer you is this (and you will thank me a few months from now for giving it to you), START TRAINING YOUR PUPPY OR DOG TODAY!!

I am not saying that so you will buy this book because there are plenty of books, DVD's, training classes and at home options out there for you to use. Shoot, try a few of them because the more people you can learn from the better.

Now, let's start training!!

Puppy Potty Training

It's almost inevitable that your puppy is going to poop and pee in your house sometime after you bring them home. It's just one of those facts of life. How fast you get your puppy potty trained will be dependent upon a couple of things. Number one on the list is how quickly you want to make things happen and number two will be the age of the puppy.

An eight week old puppy is just not going to be able to hold it as long as a twelve week old puppy or a puppy that is even a little bit older.

How long is it going to take? It's going to take a couple of weeks at least. It could even take a month or longer. Once again it all depends on the age of the pup and how dedicated you intend on being.

Here are a few key moments that you should be aware of. A puppy is going to want to go potty shortly after they wake up from their nap or after they wake up in the morning. Really anytime that they wake up there is a good chance that they will have to go (hey I'm an adult and I have to go every time I wake up).

They will normally have to go again sometime after they eat and/or drink. Anywhere from five minutes to an hour after they eat or drink they are going to have to go potty. The five minutes to an hour is a pretty good estimate, you will have a better idea of when your puppy has to go after a couple of days of observation.

Here is how we potty train our puppies. We use potty pads in the beginning for those "just in case moments" (just in case I was to lazy to get up or just in case I was not paying attention). Potty pads are designed, and I don't know really how, to attract dogs or puppies to go potty on it.

We lay the potty pad by the door that we use to take them outside to do the deed. When we see that the puppy is going to go potty and we are unable to bring them outside, we get them over to that potty pad which seems to work pretty well (at least when they go on the potty pad you won't be stepping in "IT" on your way to the kitchen).

If you can set things up where you can take them outside, shortly after they eat or shortly after they wake up you will be on your way. That's what's going to get them potty trained the fastest.

So, here is what you do, after they wake up from there nap say, "Do you have to go potty? Want to go outside?" Then you take them outside.

If you are hanging around the house and you see they are going to go potty, you say, "Have to go potty?" and you take them outside.

Once you are outside and you see they are going to relieve themselves you say, "Go potty." After they go potty tell them what a good puppy they are and either let them come back in the house or let them mess around a little bit, your choice. We usually just bring them back into the house.

Your pup will have a tell tale sign that they are about to "go" that you can keep an eye out for. Every puppy is going to be a little different, but a majority of them do the same thing. Some will just walk along sniffing the ground, if you see them do this there is a pretty good chance that they have to go.

Another tell tale sign is they will walk in a circle. Let me restate that, it is almost a certainty that if they start walking in a circle and sniffing they are going to go. So, do not hesitate on this one because if you do you may as well go and get the paper towels because you are going to have a mess to clean up. Not only that but you will have missed a potty training opportunity.

Sometimes they give a little whine and then they go, although a little harder to figure out than the other two, with a little time and observation on your part you will understand what it means. So these are a few of the "tell tale" signs that you can use.

Puppies usually like to relieve themselves in the same spot. If you see them kind of heading for that certain area that they like to go, then you know that they probably have to go potty so you should take them out and let them go.

Don't even think about it, just go. If you hesitate and say to yourself, "does he/she really have to go?" You have probably just run out of time and it is too late.

If you do miss some of these golden opportunities for a potty training lesson don't worry about it because they will still get potty trained it's just going to take a little bit longer.

I know some people talk about crate training as their potty training method of choice. They say it works pretty well and I can kind of see it, a little bit. "They are not going to pee where they sleep" they say. Well, in the beginning they are going to potty where they sleep because they aren't going to be able help it.

Puppies are just like people, we all learn through repetition. Most of us like to be on some sort of schedule. Here is an example:

Let's say you normally wake up at 6:00, 8:00 maybe 3:00 or whenever. If you begin taking your puppy out to go potty when "YOU" wake up they will begin to learn "YOUR" schedule and will normally start holding it because they will know they get to go outside and relieve themselves at a certain time.

As your pup gets older and can hold it for longer periods of time then it will be ok to hit the snooze button, but until then you need to get up out of bed and get them outside. If it's one of those days and you just don't feel like getting up then that is where the potty pad comes in. They are going to go and use it and it won't be that big a deal. It's just handy.

It is our experience that newspapers don't work very well as a form of potty training. It's one of those things that puppies just love to tear up for some reason. If you do decide to use them you need to understand that it is just a matter of time before they start ripping them up.

And for the people that say, "Oh, you know if a puppy gets used to going on a potty pad you will never get them potty trained" then I say "phooey". The potty pad is just a safety net. It's there if you're not around, if you're not paying attention, or if you just don't want to get up off of the couch and take them out. That's when it comes in handy and besides, you're not going to need it forever because the older they get the longer they can hold it.

Let's talk a little bit about your puppies feeding schedule which also makes a big difference with potty training. We usually put food out in the morning and if they eat it all, we will give them some later in the day. If you feed your puppy 2 or 3 meals a day you may have to tweak the time of their last meal of the day.

If they have difficulty holding it until morning then you will have to give them their last meal of the day a little earlier (this goes for water also), just keep a note of the time and then adjust accordingly.

The last reminder that I would like to give you on this subject of potty training is the more committed you are to house training your puppy the sooner they will become house trained.

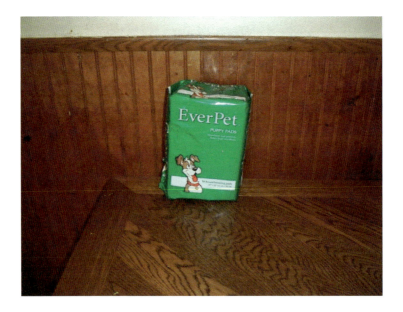

How To Stop Puppy Biting

When it comes to puppy biting you should know that most of the time they are just playing, they are not really trying to bite or hurt anybody. They are just trying to have a good time. They are young and they don't know any better. Now that being said, if they happen to hit some skin it is going to hurt whether they mean it or not.

When they bite your sock, pant leg or something like that, you want to be careful not to jerk away too suddenly. Your puppy could have his/her tooth hooked in the sock or pant leg and there is an outside chance that you could pull the puppies teeth out. That will be painful for the puppy and could require a Vet and cost extra money. Just be aware that's all I am saying.

What we do when they bite is say "AHHHH" and then reach down and tap them lightly on the bridge of their nose while saying "No."

When they bite again, and they will, just repeat the process of "AHHH". Lightly tap (DO NOT HIT) them across the bridge of the nose and say, "No." Never hesitate!!! You have to be firm when saying "No", every single time.

The other option when they start biting your hand or your leg is say "AHHH" and then reach down and hold their muzzle closed while looking them in the eye and say "NO" "No Bite".

I know some people say that you are supposed to howler and it will startle them. Well yes it is going to startle them, but it's not really going to fix the problem. You are just scaring them. You are not fixing the problem. When you tap them across the nose lightly and say, "No" or hold their muzzle shut and say, "No" it will not be fun for them anymore. Up until now, biting has been a good time, you just have to make it uncomfortable for them and that will stop the biting.

You always have to stay on top of things. You cannot let things slide, not even one time. I know they are having fun and they do not mean to hurt you but you have to correct them and you have to correct them immediately every single time.

I know they are cute, but if you begin to let them get away with stuff you will eventually begin to lose control and the last thing you want is a dog to be in charge of your life. It's no fun; I'm here to tell you it is no fun. Get on top of it and get on it early. And please don't hit them. Just lightly tap them and if that doesn't work just be a little more firm.

By staying consistent it won't take that long to teach them not to bite, it should be just a matter of time when they start to bite and they hear you say "AHHH" that will probably be the end of it, they will stop what they are doing.

While we are on the subject of the word "AHHH" you can use any word "AH AH", "IEEE" or make something up. This particular word will be used whenever you do not want them to do something, whether it is getting on the couch, jumping up on somebody or chasing the cat.

They won't understand it right away but if you use that one word every single time before you correct them for a bad behavior they will begin to understand what that word means, they will stop the bad behavior without a correction and life will become a bowl of cherries (well, maybe not a bowl of cherries but it should be much easier).

How To Stop Puppy Chewing

What puppy owner has not lost a shoe, sock or book to the chewing habits of a puppy? If you are one of these puppy owners whose puppy has already started chewing on everything, then the following advice should help you out, and if you are fortunate enough that your puppy has not started chewing "yet" then you found this book just in time.

The first thing that you need to do is get variety of chew toys. We are pretty big fans of chew ropes, but every puppy is different so you will want to have a squeaky toy or two, Kong's work pretty, well but we usually like to use them for more advanced obedience training.

We used to use rawhides which they really enjoy but sometimes after they had been chewed on for awhile they would get stuck to the roof of their mouth. No harm ever came to the pups, but they would panic a little bit until they could get it out. I am not saying don't use them, I'm saying we don't use them anymore. There are plenty of chew toys out there to choose from, you should get 4 or 5 different kinds and experiment a little bit.

The method used to stop a puppy from chewing is very similar to the one used to stop a puppy from biting.

When you see your pup chewing on something they shouldn't be you need to say "AHHH" or whatever your chosen warning word is, walk over to them, lightly tap them on the muzzle, firmly say "NO, NO CHEW" give them a chew toy and as soon as they touch it tell them what a good pup they are.

When they begin chewing on something again, and they most likely will, repeat the process of the warning word ("AHHH"), followed by a slightly firmer tap on the muzzle, then "NO, NO CHEW", offer them their toy and as they take it, tell them what a good pup they are.

If you have already begun using your "AHHH" word (or whatever warning word you have chosen) with biting or whatever undesirable behavior problem your puppy may have, they should already have a little understanding of what that word means. It's all about repetition.

You have to stay on top of it and be consistent. We talked about it in potty training and a little bit in biting. You cannot let them get away with it. If you see them chewing on anything you have to take action immediately.

One other thing that you need to be aware of is that puppies go through a teething process and that is where the chew toys will really come in handy. Chewing on something helps relieve the pain.

Leash Training A Puppy

Leash training is a fairly simple process and shouldn't take more than a few days for your pup to get the hang of it. Here is how we do it.

Before we begin getting them used to a leash, we first get them used to a collar. Get yourself a flat collar with a buckle and put it on them. You want to be able to slide two fingers underneath the collar and the puppy's neck.

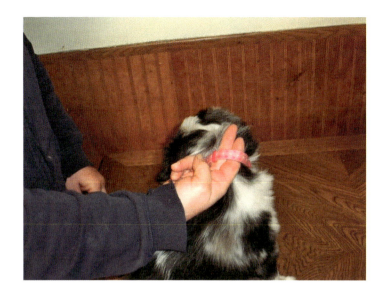

The collar needs to be tight enough so when you first start walking them with the leash they will be unable to back out of the collar (they may fight the leash a little bit and slip through the collar which you do not want to happen). Just make sure it is not too tight.

They probably won't like the collar and will more than likely spend quite a bit of their time scratching at it hoping that it will magically fall off. Let them wear it around for a few hours each day. Do this for a couple of days until they get used to it.

Now for the leash, put it on and let them drag it around for 15 or 20 minutes a couple times a day for a few days. This can be done while in the house or out in the yard, but make sure you never leave your puppy unsupervised in this situation. The last thing that you want to happen is for some type of mini disaster to occur which would set things back quite a few days.

I know that it seems like the leash training process is moving along rather slow but it really isn't.

Now it's time to attach the leash to the collar and start training. We recommend a 6 ft. leash. This is a good length as it allows your pup a little freedom but not so much freedom that they can get themselves into trouble.

Now that the leash is attached you can just start walking around. Move at a nice even pace while encouraging your pup to keep up.

When they begin to fight and pull back (and they will), stay strong and just keep slowly strolling along. It will probably take a few days but it won't be long and they will be leash trained. It does sound easy doesn't it? It really is.

Keep in mind that you don't have to do it this way. You can just go ahead and put the collar and leash on your pup, then just start walking. But, if you do and there are some people around please make sure that you charge some sort of admission because it's probably going to be a circus.

As a rule we like to get our puppies started heeling off leash before we begin the leash training but either way works fine. We will cover heeling in the next chapter.

Teaching Your Puppy To Heal

When starting to teach a puppy how to heel try to find a treat that they really enjoy, something that really excites them. We have found that most dogs and puppies really like hot dogs.

A couple of days before you start teaching your puppy to heel you want to start giving them that certain treat. You want to make sure that they really like whatever you are offering them.

Whatever this "special treat" turns out to be should only be used for training purposes and nothing else. You will also want to avoid feeding them before any practice sessions because you want them to be hungry and craving their treats.

When you begin training a puppy, one or two hot dogs (or whatever your pups chosen treat is) per training session will probably be enough. Cut the hot dogs up into little pieces as shown in the picture.

Have your puppy on your left side and hold the hot dogs in your left hand. Say heel and start walking. Place your left hand in front of your knee above your puppies head.

As you are walking along with the hot dog in your left hand you'll want to continue encouraging your puppy while feeding them the hot dogs. Think of yourself as a human Pez dispenser, the more treats the puppy receives in the beginning the happier they will be heeling beside you. You also always want to stay upbeat and happy.

When you practice heeling you'll want to walk at a fairly brisk pace, not so fast that they have to run to keep up, but not so slow that everybody gets lazy.

When you practice heeling, whether it be in the house or out in the yard it is best to walk in big circles in both directions. After you have walked a little ways (100 to 200 feet) you can "release your pup", tell them what a good puppy they are, praise them a little bit and once they have had a little time without heeling, start heeling again.

Let me quickly explain the term "release your pup" or "release your dog". This is when you allow them a few moments of free time. This is fun time where they are able to relax and play for a few seconds or to have a few treats.

The word that we use when we release our dogs is "OK". Some people just say "release" and some say "alright". Find yourself a "word" that you will use. Only use "that word" every time you take a break from practice.

And as always, practice, practice, practice.

After a couple days of heeling, you can begin to incorporate the sit which is in the next chapter.

Teaching Your Puppy To Sit

We like to start teaching our puppies to sit while we are practicing the heeling. This is just a personal preference. As you're heeling your puppy (with your pup's favorite treat in your left hand) slowly come to a stop.

At the same time that you come to a stop, say "sit" and bring your hand with the treat in it up above your pups head and slightly back which will in turn cause your puppy to sit. The pup may back up a couple of steps before he/she sits but don't worry about it, they will eventually learn to sit as soon as you come to a halt.

If you don't want to do it that way or if it doesn't seem to be working very well for you then you can do it this way. Get down on your knees (or knee). Then lightly place one hand on your puppies hind end, while holding the treat in your other hand just in front of the puppy's nose, say sit and raise the treat up and back over the puppies head while keeping pressure on his hind end. Repeat the process several times a day until the pup gets the hang of it, it shouldn't take long.

Always remember that whenever they accomplish a task to give them lots of praise and some treats, let them know what a good job they have done.

Teaching Your Puppy To Lie Down

When teaching your puppy to lie down it is best to have them in the sit position before you begin. Teaching your puppy the down can be rather difficult. For many puppies and dogs the down is a submissive behavior and the stronger willed dogs that want to be more dominant will be even more difficult to teach the down to. So please take your time and do not get discouraged.

Place your pup in the sit position with a treat in one hand and your other hand behind their shoulders. Place the hand with the treat in it in front of the puppy's nose and bring it towards the ground and forward while saying "down". If they do not want to lie down, you may have to put a little downward pressure on their shoulder blades while giving the down command. Practice this a few times a day every day until they get the hang of it.

If this method doesn't seem to be working well for you then here is another way to do it. Put them in the sit position. Place one hand behind their shoulder and place your other hand behind their front legs (as shown in the picture below). Say "down" and physically bring their legs forward with the one hand while applying light downward pressure with the other. Once they reach the down position tell them what a good pup they are and give them their treat.

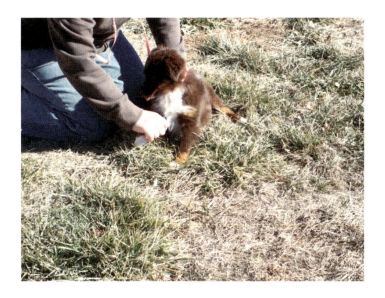

There is one other method for teaching a puppy to lie down that is a little more difficult for them to learn. Some people also claim that it can be hard on the puppy physically. We will show it to you anyway, because some puppies and dogs take to it right away. Whether it is hard on them physically or not I cannot say.

I do not use this method very often but I have in the past and no doubt will again sometime in the future.

While your puppy is standing hold the treat in one hand directly in front of the puppy's nose. Keep your hand closed just enough so they are unable to take it from your hand. Bring your hand down and back between their front legs while giving the "down" command.

As your puppy begins to walk backwards, continue to move your hand with the treat in it backwards right along with them and they will eventually lie down.

Again this technique is a little more difficult to teach. We just thought that we would add it as another option (it is even a little difficult getting still photos of the procedure).

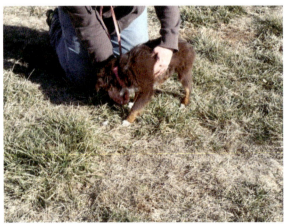

Practice a few times every day and they will eventually get the hang of it.

Teaching Your Puppy To Come

One very important thing to keep in mind when teaching your puppy to come is never ever call them to you and punish them. If you do that very often it won't be long and they will never come when called for fear of being punished. If you feel the need to get after them for something they are doing wrong then you must go to them.

To begin, you'll want to have some treats that your puppy really loves and you will want to be in a controlled environment away from any distractions. It is imperative that you try to set things up so that you will always be successful.

When your pup is just a few feet away from you call their name and when they look at you say "come" with plenty of enthusiasm. As they begin to come towards you hold both hands out in front of you with your treats in your hands, as they get closer pull your hands towards you and up towards your belly button and then give them the treats.

Try to do this a few times a day, doesn't have to be very many times just try to spread the practice sessions out a little bit.

When they have a pretty good understanding what it means when you tell them to come, have a helper hold your pup, walk about 50 or 60 ft away from your pup and start calling them, again with plenty of enthusiasm.
When you see that the puppy is struggling to get away from the helper to come to you, have them release the pup. When the pup gets to you give them lots of praise and their reward.

When I mention setting things up for success I mean you never want to give a command more than once, especially the come command. The reason for that is if your puppy happens to be headed for the road with oncoming traffic, you want them to respond the very first time you say their name and tell them to come.

If they get used to you saying Fido come, come here Fido, Fido come here, they will begin to think that is the command and by then it will be too late, damage will have been done. Now this example may be a little extreme but it is a possibility.

If you are put in a position where you have to call your pup and they do not come, you should go to them in a calm and cool manner, put your leash on them and then repeat the command and then guide them to you.

As your puppy begins to really understand what the word come means, you can then begin to lengthen the distance between you and your pup when you call them. When you believe that your puppy has a pretty reliable recall then you can begin to add distractions to the mix.

Teaching Your Puppy To Stay

For most of the other commands, when the puppy does what we ask of them, we always tell them what a good job they did in an upbeat and excited manner while giving them their treat.

When we are teaching a puppy or dog to stay we want them to remain low key. In the beginning staying still in one position for very long is difficult and the more excited or excitable a puppy (or dog) is the harder it is for them to remain in the stay position.

To begin, place your puppy in the sit position. Hold your hand in front of their face and say "stay", step right in front of your puppy, stand 20 to 30 seconds or so and then calmly step back beside them. Release your puppy but do it calmly and give them a treat. Practice this between 3 and 5 times (more or less) for a couple of days.

When your puppy breaks the stay command, and they eventually will, say "AHHH", calmly walk back to them and put them right back in the spot they were in, repeat the stay command and step back in front of them.

Gradually extend the time and the distance of the stay. Go to the end of your leash for a minute or so. When they are fairly solid at that distance drop the leash and then go 20 feet or more and so on and so on.

If they ever break the stay command after you have extended the time and or distance, it just means that you are either too far away or have made them stay for longer than they are used to. When this happens, after the correction has been made, just shorten the distance or time back up and go from there.

As with all of the other commands that you have taught your puppy, in the beginning you want to do this in a controlled environment away from all distractions. When you are confident they have a pretty solid stay then have a helper start throwing a ball around or just stroll around them making a little commotion.

Given enough practice and time you should be able to leave your dog just about any place you like for 5 minutes, 10 minutes or even much longer and not have to worry about them going anywhere. It's going to take a while before they get to that point but they will.

Our goal is to not put them in a position to fail but to always try to keep improving.

In Closing

You can always find time to work in a little practice. While cooking supper you can practice the sit and stay. If you are a big television fan you can practice a few different commands during commercials.

Both you and your pup will have days where it does not seem like things are going well. I know that there are times when I am working with a pup where I will come in and tell my family how great the pup did and the next day when we practice it felt like a complete disaster.

If the training session does not appear to be going well just stop, no big deal you can just work on it again tomorrow.

NEVER train your puppy when you are in a bad mood. It is hard to stay upbeat and enthusiastic when you are having a rough day and many people who are in a bad mood are usually looking for a reason to fly off the handle. There is no sense taking things out on your pup.

Try to end every practice session on a high note, let them believe that they are the greatest puppy on the planet.

If you start working with your pup today and try to get a little practice time in as many days a week as possible, 6 months from now you will be so much happier than if you didn't.

And what happens a year from now if you start training your puppy today? Well, everybody on the block is going to be telling you how cool you and your dog are. You will love it!!!

About The Author
Emily Pruitt

Emily's purpose in life is to help as many people as she can while she is here. She hopes that this book will help improve the relationship between you and your dog.

Never stop learning. If you would like some FREE dog training books then you can get them here http://pruittsyorkiepuppiesforsale.com/ No strings attatched!!

Made in the USA
Lexington, KY
11 September 2013